W9-BUB-366

3 1180 00557 7981

LIVING WITH JUVENILE RHEUMATOID ARTHRITIS

by Susan H. Gray

THE CHILD'S WORLD®

CHANHASSEN, MINNESOTA

*The publisher wishes to sincerely thank Courtney Bell, R.D., L.D., C.D.E.,
who herself is Living Well with JRA, for her help in preparing this book for publication.*

Published in the United States of America by The Child's World®
P.O. Box 326
Chanhassen, MN 55317-0326
800-599-READ
www.childsworld.com

Photo Credits: Cover: Nicole Katano/Brand X Pictures/Corbis, Custom Medical Stock Photo,
Inc., (inset); Bettmann/Corbis: 22 (top); Randy Faris/Corbis: 22 (bottom); Nicole
Katano/Brand X Pictures/Corbis: 1; Science Pictures Limited/Corbis: 12; Custom Medical
Stock Photo, Inc.: 6, 7, 10, 13, 20; The Image Bank/GettyImages: 19; Stone/GettyImages: 9,
11, 15, 29; Susan Gray: 23; Tami Payton: 24, 26; Cindy Charles/PhotoEdit: 27; Myrleen
Ferguson 16; Tony Freeman: 18; Bonnie Kamin: 17; Michael Newman: 8; David Young-
Wolff: 14; Erin Garvey/Courtesy of the Silver Ring Company: 25; Nancy P.
Alexander/Unicorn Stock Photos: 5

The Child's World®: Mary Berendes, Publishing Director

Editorial Directions, Inc.: E. Russell Primm, Editor; Alice Flanagan, Photo Researcher; Linda
S. Koutris, Photo Selector; The Design Lab, Designer and Page Production; Red Line
Editorial, Fact Researcher; Irene Keller, Copy Editor; Tim Griffin/IndexServ, Indexer; Donna
Frassetto, Proofreader

Library of Congress Cataloging-in-Publication Data
Gray, Susan H.
 Living with juvenile rheumatoid arthritis / by Susan H. Gray.
   v. cm.— (Living Well series)
Includes index.
Contents: Benny's story—What is juvenile rheumatoid arthritis?—What causes JRA?—What's
it like to live with this disease?—How do we know about JRA?—How do we help people with
JRA today?—What are we learning now?
 ISBN 1-56766-104-1
1. Rheumatoid arthritis in children—Juvenile literature. [1. Rheumatoid arthritis. 2. Arthritis.
3. Diseases.] I. Title. II. Series.
 RJ482.A77 G73 2002
  618.92'7227—dc21   2002002870

TABLE OF CONTENTS

CHAPTER ONE

DO YOU KNOW SOMEONE WHO HAS JUVENILE RHEUMATOID ARTHRITIS?

Benny hears his mother calling him to wake up. The school bus will be arriving soon. Benny loves school and he can't wait to see his friend David. But Benny hates to get up. His knees hurt so much that he doesn't want to get out of bed. Slowly he rolls out, and he painfully walks to the bathroom. After a hot shower, he feels a lot better. But it still hurts him to walk down the stairs for breakfast.

Benny is one of about 285,000 children in the United States with arthritis (ar-THRY-tiss). The most common kind of arthritis in children is called juvenile rheumatoid (JOO-vuh-nyl ROO-muh-toyd) arthritis. It affects 50,000 kids—about one in every 5,700 persons. Juvenile rheumatoid arthritis is called JRA for short.

JRA is often most painful first thing in the morning.

CHAPTER TWO

WHAT IS JRA?

The word *juvenile* tells you that JRA affects children or young

people. *Rheumatoid* comes from a Latin word that means "to hurt."

Arthritis comes from a Greek word meaning "joint." Joints are places

where two bones come together. Shoulders, knees, elbows, and ankles

are joints. So juvenile rheumatoid

arthritis is a disease that causes

children to feel pain in their joints.

JRA affects children under 16.

Girls get it more often than boys do.

It causes joints to swell, stiffen, and

be very painful. Many other things

could hurt joints, of course. One

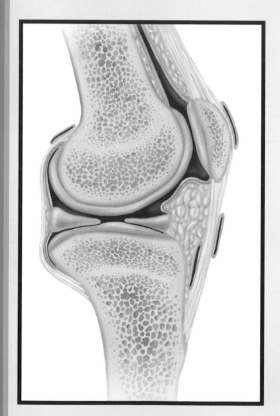

An illustration of a knee joint

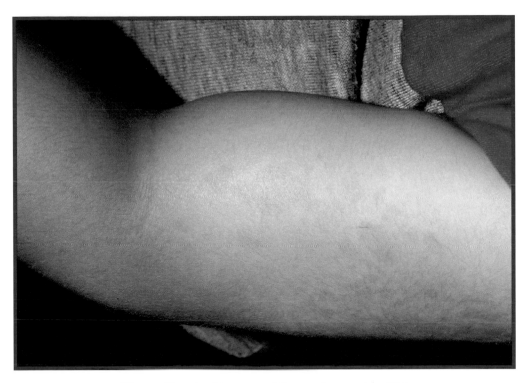

The swelling in this young girl's arm is caused by JRA.

thing that could make a joint act this way, for example, is a sports

injury. But when such problems last for six weeks or longer, doctors

start checking for JRA.

There are three types of JRA. About half the children have

pauciarticular (paw-see-ar-TIK-yoo-lur) JRA. That means they have

problems with up to four joints. Usually, these are large joints such as

the knees. Some kids with this kind of JRA also have eye problems.

A doctor checks the eyes of a young girl with JRA.

They need to visit an eye doctor every few months. They also might

need eyedrops.

The second kind of JRA is polyarticular (paw-lee-ar-TIK-yoo-

lur). This type affects five joints or more. Usually these are small

joints, such as those in the hands and feet.

The third kind is systemic (sis-TEM-ik). Systemic JRA affects many parts of the body. Joints swell up and hurt. Fevers come and

go. Rashes appear on the skin. There might even be problems with

the heart or liver.

Children with JRA have painful joints when they wake up in

the morning, like Benny. As they move around more, they start to

feel better. Sometimes JRA disappears for months, and the joints

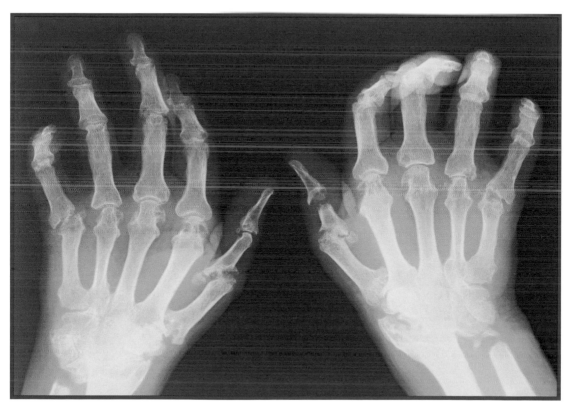

This X ray shows the hands of an elderly person who suffers from arthritis.

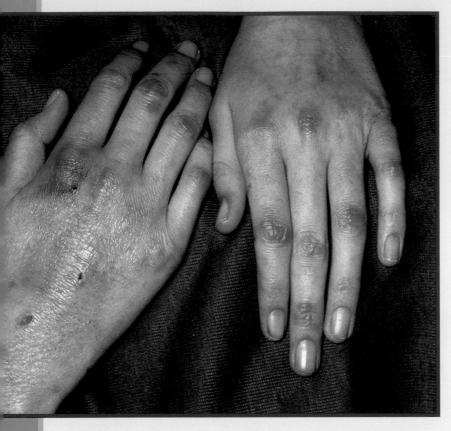

Rashes sometimes appear on the skin of people with JRA.

feel fine. Then it suddenly comes back in what is called a flare, or a flare-up.

JRA can be mild or very severe. A child may have it for a couple of months, and then it may go away for the rest of his or her life. Another child may have JRA for years on end. As this child gets older, his or her joints might not grow evenly. One arm could grow a little longer than the other. One knee might be crooked. He or she might limp when walking. He or she may not grow as tall as other children. Luckily, most kids outgrow the disease.

CHAPTER THREE

WHAT CAUSES JRA?

A problem with the body's immune (ih-MYOON) system causes juvenile rheumatoid arthritis. Your immune system helps your body fight sickness. Germs such as bacteria and viruses can make you sick. When they enter the body, the immune system goes to work. It sends out **white blood cells** to attack and destroy the germs.

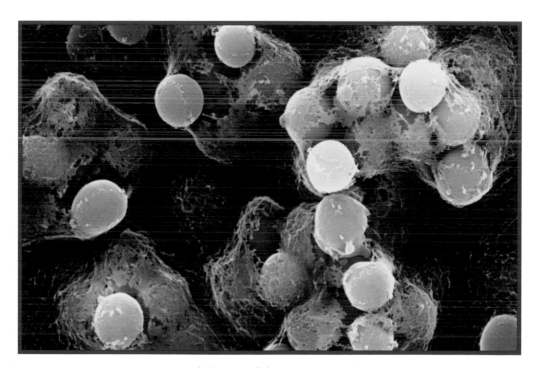

A magnified view of the streptococcus bacteria

In a child with JRA, however, the immune system makes a

mistake. It sends out white cells to attack healthy joints and organs.

The white cells try to destroy the normal tissues there. This makes

the joints hurt

and swell up.

No one is

sure why things go

wrong like this.

Doctors think

some children

A magnified view of human blood cells

might have **genes** for the disease. A child could be fine for a

while. Then something in his or her **environment** wakes the

immune system, and it attacks the joints. The child then has JRA.

It is not easy for doctors to know if someone has this disease.

Doctors must look for several things. A child who limps in the morning or after a nap could have JRA. A child with joints that stay swollen for weeks could have it. A child with high fevers that come and go could have systemic JRA. A child with JRA might have joint damage that shows up in X rays.

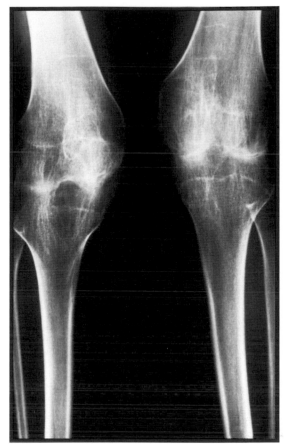

An X ray of a patient with JRA in the knees

The problem is that other things could cause these problems, too. Doctors want to be sure their **diagnosis** is correct, so they may watch a child for months. While they are watching, the disease could go away completely. Then no one would ever know if it was JRA or not.

CHAPTER FOUR

What's It Like to Live with JRA?

With juvenile rheumatoid arthritis, it can be hard just to get up in the morning. Joints hurt and are very stiff. Many children find that sleeping under a warm electric blanket helps. Some like a hot shower as soon as they get up. Then as they move around during the day, they feel better.

Stiff joints in the morning can make filling the tub with water painful. The warm water, however, will help this girl feel better.

Getting ready for school can be tough. A child with JRA feels pain when he or she gets dressed. Even tying a shoe is hard and painful.

When you have JRA, brushing your teeth can make your jaws ache.

His or her hands hurt while eating breakfast. Brushing one's teeth

makes the jaws ache. He or she can't move around much on the school

bus, so a child with JRA is often stiff when he or she gets to school.

At school, a girl with JRA might have trouble writing or

drawing because her hands hurt. She might not want to stand up

because her knees are sore. She might have trouble seeing the teacher

Because JRA can sometimes affect eyesight, class work can be more difficult.

because of her eye problems. At recess, she might not run because she feels clumsy and doesn't want the other kids to laugh at her.

People often think that children with JRA are faking their pain. The children act like their joints are aching in the morning. Then they seem okay in the afternoon. Their pain is real, though. Later in the day, they often feel better. This is because they have exercised their joints, and moving the joints made them feel better.

Kids with JRA have to put up with a lot of things. Sometimes other kids are rude or stare at them. Sometimes grown-ups treat

Good friends always make recess easier and more fun.

them like they are not very smart. As a result, good friends are

especially important to kids with JRA. Friends help by eating with

them in the cafeteria. Friends play with them at recess. The very best

friends pick them to be on their teams.

Summer camp is a chance to be outside and learn new things, such as how to swim.

Many states have summer camps for children with arthritis. At camp, kids with JRA learn to swim and canoe and do crafts. And they never have to worry about being different or having people laugh at them.

CHAPTER FIVE

WHAT CAN WE
DO ABOUT JRA?

People have had joint problems since **ancient** times. Signs of

arthritis have been found in

Egyptian mummies. Long

ago, people believed that

evil fluids in the body

caused arthritis.

Over the years, all

kinds of cures have been

suggested. Some people

tried drinking vinegar.

Some tried pulling out

their teeth. Some people let

Scientists have found arthritis in ancient Egyptian mummies.

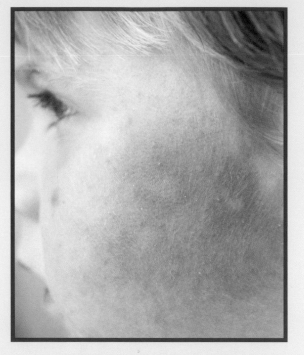
People used to believe a bee sting would help with the pain of arthritis.

bees sting them—on purpose. In ancient Rome, a doctor told his arthritis patients to go swimming in the sea. He said they should put their feet on a torpedo fish as it swam by and the fish would give them electric shocks. The doctor claimed the electric shocks would cure their arthritis. Of course, none of these things worked. Arthritis remained a mystery for thousands of years.

Then, in the 1890s, a doctor in England got interested. He studied children with arthritis. His name was George Still. Today, systemic JRA is also called "Still's disease."

In the 1940s, more doctors became interested. Many thought

that children with JRA should just stay in hospitals. In time, they

saw that this was a bad idea. They started working on better ways to

help the children, like **therapy** (THER-uh-pee) and exercise.

Now doctors can tell when someone has juvenile rheumatoid

THE GIRL BY THE LAKE

In the 1930s, scientists in Louisiana discovered an ancient village and graveyard. The scientists were fascinated by what they found. As they explored the area, they found old dishes and tools. They dug up arrowheads, jewelry, and human skeletons. They also found shells, so they knew that the humans had lived near a lake.

The scientists also found the bones of a little girl. Her joints were larger than usual. Other scientists took a look at the bones. They decided she may have had JRA. The little girl's knees probably hurt as she gathered shells. She probably had a hard time keeping up with her friends. That little girl died before she outgrew her arthritis, but that was 2,500 years ago. Her family never knew what her problem was or how they could help her.

arthritis. They know the three different kinds of the disease. They know lots of ways to help their patients.

Today, doctors have medicines and operations that are helpful. Many children take aspirin or ibuprofen for their pain. Some need stronger drugs. Children must be careful with these drugs because they can cause other problems.

Most kids with JRA just need good therapy. They need to see a

Vincent du Vigneaud (above top) won the Nobel Prize in chemistry in 1955 for his work on finding a treatment for rheumatoid arthritis. Aspirin (above bottom) often helps with JRA pain.

physical therapist (FIZZ-uh-kuhl THER-uh-pist) or an occupational (ahk-yoo-PAY-shuhn-uhl) therapist. These therapists show patients how to do things better. Physical therapists teach their patients special exercises. The exercises strengthen the muscles and

A physical therapist works with a child in a swimming pool.

help the stiff joints to move. Children need to exercise their joints often, or the pain and stiffness get worse. Someone who has been sick for a while has probably not exercised. The physical therapist can help him get back in shape.

Occupational therapists help patients learn how to do everyday tasks.

Occupational therapists help kids with everyday tasks, such as writing and brushing their teeth. They show children how to use special grips on their pencils. They might suggest getting an electric toothbrush. Therapists also show children the best positions to use in their naps. Getting into the right positions keeps joints from hurting when the children wake up.

When bad flare-ups come, it's probably best not to move the joints much. It is just too painful. Flare-ups usually last a few days. Afterwards, the joints are stiff again, and the exercises have to start all over.

Physical and occupational therapists make splints for their patients. Splints are stiff pieces of plastic or metal. Children wear the splints

An in-line skater wears ring splints to help lessen joint pain.

around their hurt joints. Splints hold the joints in the proper position. If joints are growing crooked, splints pull them back in line. Some splints are big enough to fit on the legs. Some are small enough to fit on the fingers. They are called ring splints.

A young girl learns how to wear her arm splint.

Usually, children wear splints only at night. During the day,

their joints need to move. Therapists make special splints for each

child. As the child grows, the therapist makes new splints.

CHAPTER SIX

WILL WE EVER CURE JRA?

Today, many scientists are trying to learn more about JRA. Some are studying how genes work. Others are trying to find out what in the environment triggers a flare-up. Still others are trying to find out why the immune system attacks the joints.

Some doctors are working on better drugs. When they think they have a good, new drug they test it on people. A few years ago, doctors tried a new drug on more than 1,000 people with arthritis. Some of them were children with JRA. The drug seemed to work well, and the children had fewer flare-ups. So children have helped doctors to learn about this disease. Maybe someday, children will help find the cure.

Research is continuing to find a cure for JRA.

Glossary

ancient (AYN-shunt) Something ancient is something very old.

diagnosis (dye-uhg-NOH-siss) A diagnosis identifies a disease by its symptoms.

environment (en-VYE-ruhn-ment) Our environment is made up of everything around us.

genes (JEENS) Genes are the parts of cells that decide which features of the parents a child will inherit.

therapy (THER-uh-pee) Therapy is the treatment of an illness or problem.

white blood cells (WITE BLUHD SELS) White blood cells are tiny cells in the bloodstream that normally fight disease.

Questions and Answers about JRA

Will somebody with JRA ever get better? About seven out of every ten kids with JRA will grow out of it. The others can learn which exercises and medicines make them feel better.

Can I catch JRA from someone else? You could never catch JRA from someone else. It's okay to share your toys or spend the night with a friend who has JRA.

A boy at my school has JRA. What can I do to help him? Watch and see what he has trouble with. Maybe he has trouble opening his milk carton. You could help him with that, and then stay and eat lunch with him.

Will it hurt him to play? He probably does not need to play rough games like football. But sports such as softball, swimming, and kickball could be okay.

What's the hardest part of having this disease? There are several hard parts. Children with JRA may have trouble walking and running. Some kids don't want to play with them. Some people stare at them and even may talk about them behind their backs. This is hurtful and makes children with JRA feel embarrassed. Another hard part is that kids never know when a flare-up might come. They might plan on going to a birthday party next week. Then they get a flare-up and are in too much pain to go.

Helping a Friend Who Has JRA

Children with JRA are often afraid no one will play or eat with them at school. If you have a friend with JRA, be sure to sit with her at lunch and invite some other friends to join you. At recess, play games that are not too rough so your friend can join in. Children with JRA might like basketball, baseball, kickball, or hopscotch. They might want to help build a fort or play on the playground equipment.

Did You Know?

▸ Some ring splints look like fancy silver or gold rings.

▸ Kids with JRA often soak their hands in warm, melted wax to feel better.

▸ Lyme disease seems a lot like JRA. Someone with Lyme disease can have a rash, a fever, and stiff, swollen joints. But Lyme disease is caused by tick bites.

How to Learn More about JRA

At the Library: Nonfiction

Aldape, Virginia Tortorica, and Lillian S. Kossacoff (Photographer).
Nicole's Story: A Book about a Girl with Juvenile Rheumatoid Arthritis.
Minneapolis: Lerner Publications Company, 1996.

Fall, Guy.
Everything You Need to Know about Juvenile Arthritis.
New York: Rosen Publishing Group, 2002.

Llewellyn, Claire.
Arthritis.
Mankato, Minn.: Thameside Press, 2001.

At the Library: Fiction

Kehret, Peg.
My Brother Made Me Do It.
New York: Pocket Books, 2000.

Melas, Elizabeth Murphy, and April Hartmann (Illustrator).
Keeping a Secret: A Story about Juvenile Rheumatoid Arthritis.
Albuquerque, N.M.: Health Press, 2001.

Striegel, Jana.
Homeroom Exercise.
New York: Holiday House, 2001.

Thiele, Colin.
Jody's Journey.
New York: HarperCollins, 1990.

Thiele, Colin, and John Schoenherr (Illustrator).
Storm Boy.
New York: HarperCollins Children's Books, 1978.

On the Web

Visit our home page for lots of links about JRA:
http://www.childsworld.com/links.html

Note to Parents, Teachers, and Librarians: We routinely verify our Web links to make sure they're safe, active sites—so encourage your readers to check them out!

Through the Mail or by Phone

The American College of Rheumatology
1800 Century Place, Suite 250
Atlanta, GA 30345
404/633-3777

American Juvenile Arthritis Organization (AJAO)
1330 West Peachtree Street
Atlanta, GA 30309
404/965-7514 or 800/283-7800
http://www.arthritis.org/communities/about_ajao.asp

The Arthritis Foundation
P.O. Box 7669
Atlanta, GA 30357-0669
404/872-7100

Kids on the Block, Inc.
9385-C Gerwig Lane
Columbia, MD 21046
410/290-9095

Index

About the Author

Susan H. Gray has a bachelor's degree and a master's degree in zoology. She has taught college-level biology, anatomy, and physiology classes. In her 25 years as an author, she has written medical articles, science papers, and children's books. Ms. Gray especially enjoys writing on scientific topics for children, as it is a challenge to present complex material to young readers. In addition to her children's books, she writes grant proposals for several organizations. Ms. Gray lives with her husband, Michael, in Cabot, Arkansas. She enjoys playing the piano, traveling, and gardening.